Lincoln Clears a Path

ABRAHAM LINCOLN'S AGRICULTURAL LEGACY

PEGGY THOMAS

ILLUSTRATED BY
STACY INNERST

CALKINS CREEK

AN IMPRINT OF BOYDS MILLS & KANE
New York

When the wagon stopped in the middle of
the Indiana wilderness, seven-year-old
Abe Lincoln saw only miles of dense forest.
This was not a farm.
Not yet.

First, his family needed to clear a path.

Abe helped his father fell trees.

In Lincoln's day more than half of Americans lived on farms,

Swish!

He cleared brush.

THWUMP!

He pulled stumps.

yah!

He plowed fields.

Soon they had a farm that was better than the one they left behind in Kentucky.
But farm life didn't always go smoothly.

Once, Abe planted pumpkin seeds across
seven acres of land.
  The next day a storm burst in the hills.
It flooded down the valley and washed
every . . . last . . . seed . . . away.

During the day Abe mastered "soils, seeds, and seasons—hedges, ditches, and fences."

At night he learned about stars, math and poetry—"life, liberty and the pursuit of happiness."

Abe marveled at how the founding fathers—*Thwack! Swish! Thwump! Yah!*—cleared a path for folks like him.

In many other countries, if you were born poor, you remained poor.

The Declaration of Independence gave Abe the freedom to try new things and improve his life.

At the age of twenty-one, Abe journeyed with his family
to Illinois. On a bitter March morning while crossing a stream,
the Lincolns' oxen broke through the ice.

The wagon rocked . . .

The wagon tipped . . .

But they made it across!

Then Abe looked back.

On the other side, their dog shivered and whined. Abe could not leave the poor soul behind. He pulled off his boots, and—*swish*—waded across the icy stream.

Abe tucked the pup under his arm and carried him back to the wagon.

Once his family was settled, Abe struck out on his own to float farmers' goods to market. Near New Salem, Illinois, Abe's flatboat ran aground.

Water rushed over the stern.

Thwack! Abe hurried the hogs ashore.

Swish! He rolled pork barrels forward.

Thwump! He punched a hole in the hull.

Yah! Water gushed out.

The boat lifted, and it was smooth sailing to New Orleans.

Abe traveled more than a thousand miles down the Mississippi River.

Abe said that earning his first dollar made the world seem "wider and fairer" than ever before. At least as *w-i-d-e* as the Mississippi. But . . .

Life was not *fair* to everyone.

In New Orleans, runaway slave posters plastered every wall, women in chains swept the streets, and the sickening strike of the auctioneer's gavel echoed through the alleys.

Could anyone ever clear a path for them?

More than fifty slave markets blemished the city of New Orleans.

Back in New Salem, Lincoln became a shopkeeper.

A postmaster.

A surveyor.

He always seemed happiest when solving someone else's problem. *Why don't you study law and run for office,* his friends urged.

But how?

Thwack! Swish! Thwump! Yah! His friends eased the way.
One friend shared his bunk with him.
Another helped him study math.
Others lent him books to read, and money for a suit to wear.

THWACK!

SWISH!

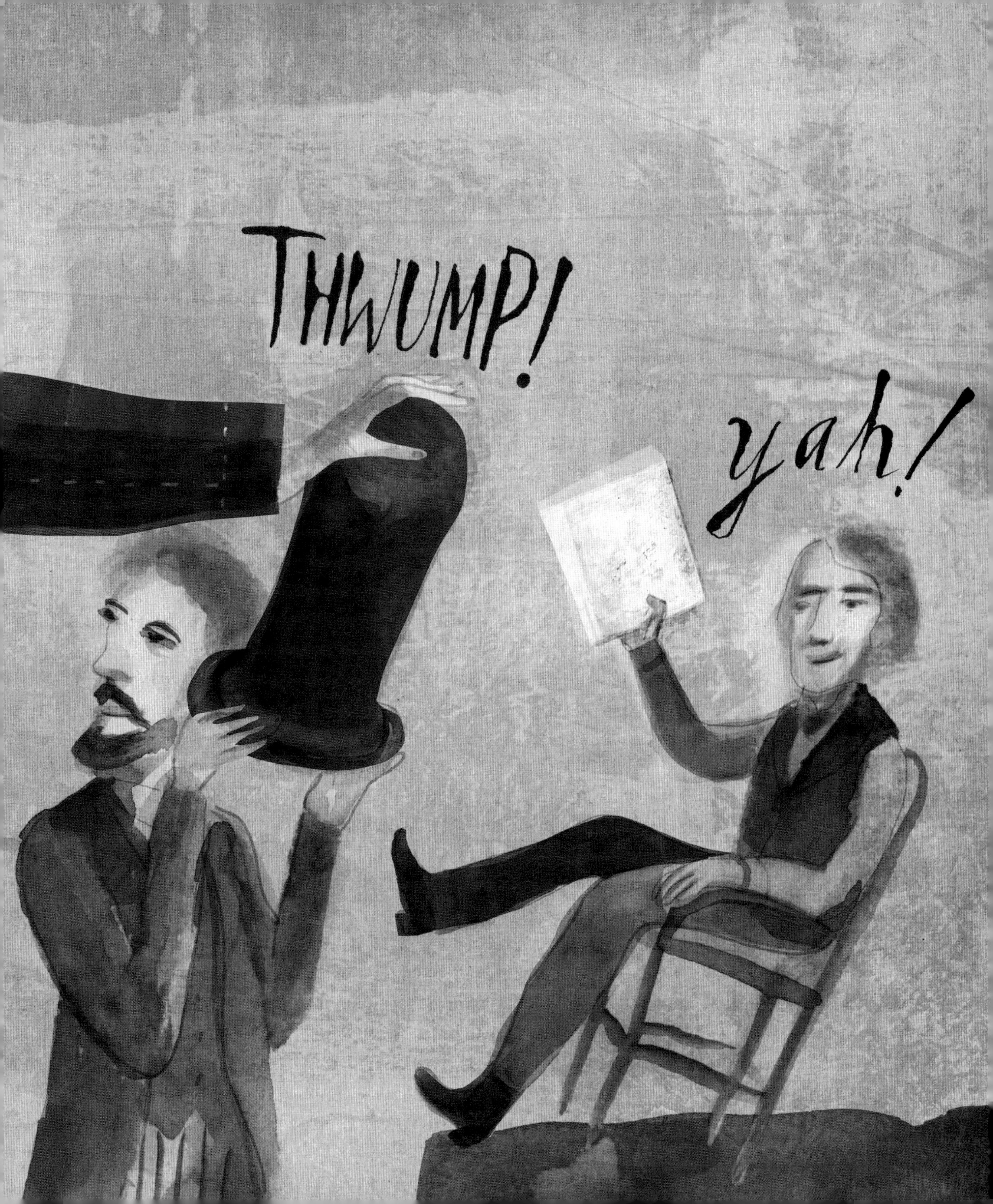
THWUMP!
yah!

By 1834, Lincoln was in the Illinois legislature. *Swish! Thwack!* He cleared a path for better schools and more roads.

"The legitimate object of government, is to do for a community of people, whatever they need to have done, but can not do, **at all**, or can not, **so well do**, for themselves."

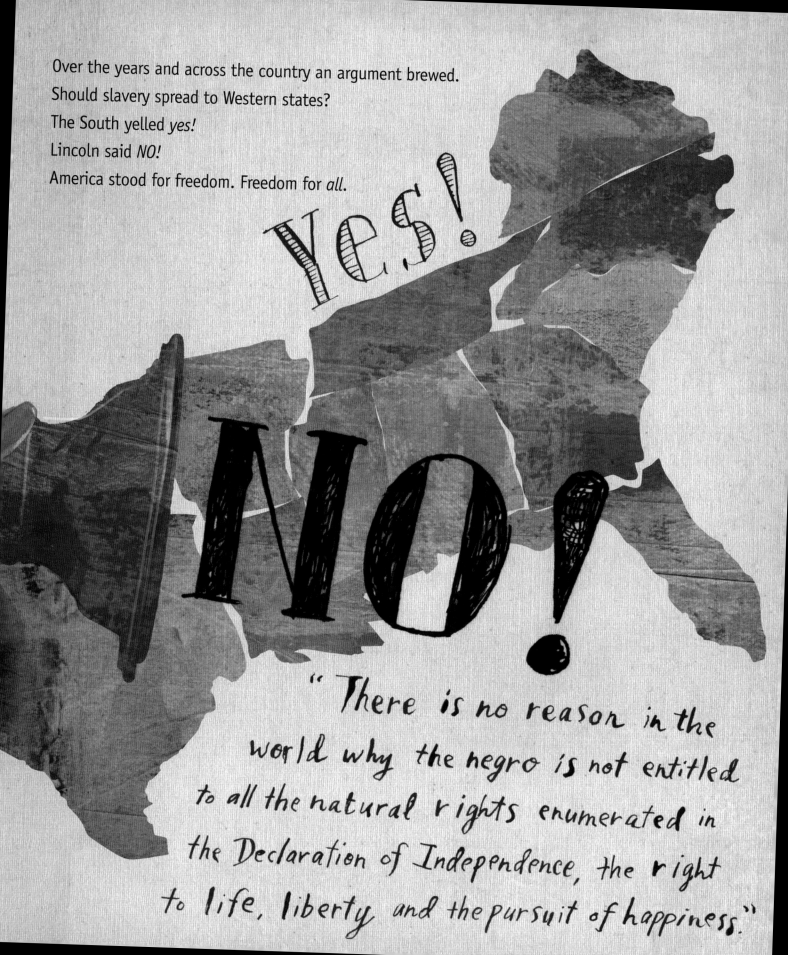

Over the years and across the country an argument brewed.
Should slavery spread to Western states?
The South yelled *yes!*
Lincoln said *NO!*
America stood for freedom. Freedom for *all.*

Yes!

NO!

"There is no reason in the world why the negro is not entitled to all the natural rights enumerated in the Declaration of Independence, the right to life, liberty, and the pursuit of happiness."

In 1860, when voters elected Lincoln president,
the country ripped in two.

Eleven Southern states left the Union
and called themselves the Confederate States of America.

The Civil War began.

Confederate soldiers fired on Union soldiers at Fort Sumter, South Carolina.

Cornfields turned into battlefields.
Defeats rolled in like an endless storm.
By 1862, the war seemed as if it would never end.

Then, Lincoln's eleven-year-old son, Willie, fell ill and died.
The president's world seemed darker than the densest forest
at midnight.

How would he get his family and
America through this heartache?

From the White House window, Lincoln could see the Washington Monument.

Unfinished, it was a sad reminder that half the nation was gone, yet—hundreds of cattle grazed in its shadow.

Wounded soldiers filled the capital, but—new recruits marched in daily.

Supply trains hurried to the front, while just as quickly, train loads of grain poured into the depot.

It wasn't just a soldiers' war. *All* Americans were in this fight. And all Americans needed hope.

Half a million men left their crops to fight. Women and children took over family farms.

Each month, farmers provided 24.3 million pounds of fresh beef, 136,994 barrels of flour, and 8.5 million pounds of potatoes.

That is why in the middle of a war, with the country divided, Lincoln lifted his pen and as surely as if he held an ax, he cleared a path for America's future.

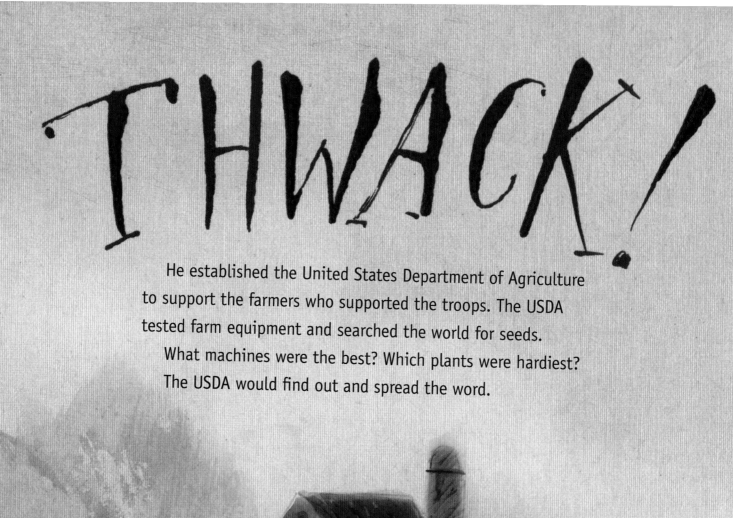

THWACK!

He established the United States Department of Agriculture
to support the farmers who supported the troops. The USDA
tested farm equipment and searched the world for seeds.
What machines were the best? Which plants were hardiest?
The USDA would find out and spread the word.

SWISH!

Lincoln signed the Homestead Act and cleared a path west.
A hundred and sixty acres to any citizen or immigrant, farmer,
or merchant, man or woman, who wanted a fair chance to make
it on their own.

"New free States are the places for poor people to go to
and better their condition."

A. Lincoln.

Lincoln hoped to populate the West with settlers who believed that slavery was wrong.

Settlers created more than a hundred thousand new farms in Nebraska alone.

THWUMP!

Lincoln signed the Pacific Railway Act and cleared a path across the nation. It sped people west and zoomed farm products east.

A. Lincoln.

The original line stretched 1,776 miles.

So many pigs rode the rails to Chicago, they called the city *Porkopolis*.

yah!

Lincoln created land-grant colleges, clearing a path for students.

"Upon the subject of education...
I can only say that I view it as
the most important subject which we
as a people can be engaged in."

A. Lincoln.

...Vermont congressman Justin Morrill.

Today there are more than a hundred land-grant colleges.

These colleges would teach agriculture because

"Every blade of grass is a study; and to produce TWO where there was but ONE, is both a profit and a pleasure. And not grass alone; but SOILS, SEEDS, and seasons — hedges, ditches, and fences, draining, drouths, and irrigation — PLOWING, HOEING, and HARROWING — reaping, mowing, and threshing — saving crops, pests of crops, diseases of crops... implements, utensils, and MACHINES... hogs, horses, and cattle — sheep, goats, and poultry — TREES, shrubs, fruits, plants, and FLOWERS... each a world of study within itself."

There was just one more obstacle for Lincoln to remove.

On January 1, 1863, Lincoln issued the Emancipation Proclamation and cleared a path to freedom.

"Liberty to all"... clears the path for all— gives hope to all."

"Let us hope...
that by the best cultivation
of the physical world,
beneath and around us,
and the intellectual and
moral world within us,
we shall secure... prosperity
and happiness... which, while the
earth endures, shall not pass away."

> "I want it said of me by those who know me best
> that I always plucked a thistle and planted a flower
> where I thought a flower would grow."

Author's Note

While researching Lincoln, I noticed that he used the phrase "clearing a path" several times in his writing. Sometimes he was referring to the removal of rocks and stumps so a wagon could pass, but other times he was thinking about ways to remove much bigger obstacles like poverty, racism, and ignorance so that all Americans could lead a better life.

We all have the ability to help others. How could you clear a path? You could clear an actual path by shoveling a neighbor's sidewalk, or maybe you could welcome a new student so it is easier for them to make new friends. Perhaps you could write a thank-you letter to someone who cleared a path for you. For more ideas go to peggythomaswrites.com, and share all the ways you, like Lincoln, have cleared a path and made the world a better place.

I'd like to thank the people who cleared a path for this book. Thank you to James M. Cornelius, PhD, curator, Lincoln Collection at the Abraham Lincoln Presidential Library & Museum; and to R. Douglas Hurt, professor of history, Purdue University, for his extensive research on American agriculture during the Civil War, and for his kind words regarding the manuscript. Thank you also to Kevin Pawlak, education specialist at Mosby Heritage Area Association for reading an early draft.

Special appreciation goes to Kevin Daugherty, director of education at Illinois Agriculture in the Classroom, for his encouragement, and to my wonderful editor Carolyn P. Yoder for her friendship and patience.

President Abraham Lincoln, 1863

Lincoln's Early Life

Lincoln was born on February 12, 1809 in central Kentucky. The family had to move in 1816, when they lost their land claim to another settler.

At the time, most people grew their own food and made their own clothes. It took hard work and determination to survive. As soon as little Abe was old enough, he fetched water, gathered kindling, picked berries, and planted seeds. When he grew tall and strong, he felled trees, split logs to make fence rails, harvested the fields, and took grain to the mill. Lincoln learned *how* to be a frontier farmer, but he admitted that he didn't learn to *love* it. He preferred to read and use his brain more than his muscles to help people. But schools were often far away or nonexistent, and Abe was needed at home during planting and harvest times. Lincoln suspected that he spent a total of one year in school. It was his stepmother who introduced him to books, which then introduced him to America's founding fathers and their ideals.

When Lincoln was twenty-one years old, he left the farm to make his own way in the world. He earned money working for other farmers, and floated produce to market on a flatboat. He ran a general store, was postmaster, learned to survey land, and was a captain during the Black Hawk War.

In 1832, he ran for Illinois state representative but failed. He won in 1834 because he supported road and river improvements. He taught himself the law and in 1837 became an attorney in Springfield. By traveling the Eighth Judicial Circuit, Lincoln kept in touch with rural life. When he stopped for the night at a farmhouse, Lincoln often sneaked out to the barn to tinker with the farming tools. His fascination with machinery came in handy when in court he represented the inventors of harvesting equipment. One time he had the whole jury on its hands and knees inspecting every wire and widget.

All of these experiences helped Lincoln become the sixteenth president of the United States. Many voters respected his frontier background, his capacity for hard work, and his desire to help people less fortunate than he was. Abraham Lincoln also never forgot the farming community of his youth or how important agriculture was (and is) to the nation's success.

As a young man, Lincoln split wood to make rails for fencing. He'd later be known as the "Rail Splitter."

Lincoln's Agricultural Legacy

In a flurry of law-making during the spring and summer of 1862, as if he knew time was limited, President Lincoln signed four key congressional acts that greatly affected American agriculture.

The Department of Agriculture Act (signed May 15, 1862)

Before the creation of the USDA, anything related to agriculture was handled by the patent office. But as Lincoln said, agriculture was "the largest interest in the nation," and should have a proper department. He appointed Isaac Newton, a dairy farmer from Pennsylvania, as the first commissioner of agriculture.

Today, the head of the USDA is called the secretary of agriculture and is part of the president's cabinet. The USDA continues to support farmers and ranchers, but also promotes trade, ensures food safety, protects natural resources, develops rural areas, and prevents hunger through its Food and Nutrition Services.

The Homestead Act (signed May 20, 1862)

Any citizen or immigrant interested in homesteading could apply to receive a hundred and sixty acres of public land. They had to be over twenty-one years of

The original building of the Department of the USDA. Located at 14th and Independence Avenue, it was common to see rows of experimental crops growing on what is now the National Mall.

age, and not have taken up arms against the Union. Settlers had to live on the land for five years and make improvements, such as building a house and planting crops, after which they owned their plot. By 1934, the government processed more than 1.6 million applications. The policy ended in 1976 in the lower forty-eight states and in 1986 in Alaska.

Although the Homestead Act was instrumental for growing the country, it ravaged Native American nations who lived on the land the government gave away. Bloody battles led to government agents rounding up tribes that had to give up their way of life and live on reservations.

The Pacific Railway Act (signed July 1, 1862)

This law funded the construction of railway and telegraph lines from the Missouri River to the Pacific Ocean. Two companies worked on the project. The Union Pacific Railroad Company worked from the Missouri moving west and the Central Pacific Railroad Company worked from San Francisco moving east. The two lines connected on May 10, 1869 in Promontory, Utah. The new railroad reduced the dangerous months-long journey in a wagon to a safer eight-day trip, and offered farmers faster transportation for their goods. However, it also accelerated Western settlement and the destruction of Native American communities.

The Morrill Act (signed July 2, 1862)

Justin Morrill, a representative from Vermont, proposed that the federal government grant each state thirty thousand acres per Congress member. The state could build a college on that land or sell the land to fund a college elsewhere. These land-grant colleges were designed to teach agriculture, engineering, and mechanical arts in order to increase American productivity. In 1890, Morrill, now a senator, proposed a second land-grant act to ensure African Americans equal access to the colleges in Southern states.

The American Agricultural Revolution

Since the availability of the mechanical reaper in 1840, farmers moved steadily from handheld tools, like the ones Lincoln used, to horse-drawn and steam-powered machines. Increasing productivity changed subsistence farming (growing one's own food) to commercial farming (selling one's produce for profit). Lincoln's four acts accelerated this transformation, and information about new inventions and methods spread more quickly with the creation of the USDA. More railroads allowed farm produce to travel farther and helped establish central distribution hubs. The Homestead Act vastly increased the number of farms, and the Morrill Act cultivated scientists who went on to introduce disease-resistant crops, develop cures for fatal livestock illnesses, and discover new uses for farm products.

The collapse of Fort Sumter in Charleston Harbor signaled the beginning of the Civil War.

The Civil War

Primary conflict: A disagreement about the kind of society that would spread into new Western states: one based on agriculture and slave labor or one based on industry and opportunity for all

North: Union; President Abraham Lincoln as commander-in-chief

South: Confederate; Jefferson Davis as commander-in-chief

Began: April 12, 1861, Confederate troops fire on Fort Sumter, South Carolina

Ended: April 9, 1865, Confederate army surrenders to Union forces at Appomattox Court House, Virginia

General Robert E. Lee signed the Confederate's surrender as Union General Ulysses S. Grant looked on.

Farmers: Soldiers in the Field

During the Civil War, Lincoln asked farmers to cultivate all the land they had to feed and supply the Union army. Even though many farmers volunteered to fight, productivity still increased. Often, mothers, sisters, and wives patriotically stepped in to take over the farming. This became so common that manufacturers of farm equipment changed their ads to show women sitting atop threshing machines.

In 1862, there were six hundred thousand military men to feed. Every month, farmers provided 48,750 bushels of beans, and 8.5 million pounds of potatoes.

The basement of the Capitol building was made into a giant bakery that turned 230 barrels of flour into sixty thousand loaves of bread a day.

The soldiers' mounts also needed to eat. The horses for just the Army of the Potomac gobbled up 125 tons of hay a day.

Every soldier also wore a wool uniform, and one estimate stated that the army would need 51 million pounds of wool each year of the war.

Even though the army consumed an enormous amount food and fiber, farmers still grew more than enough grain to send to Europe. One British official said that in one year the Union shipped enough food to feed three to four million Britons. This aid convinced the British to support the Union's cause.

During the Civil War, army cattle grazed in the shadow of the unfinished Washington Monument.

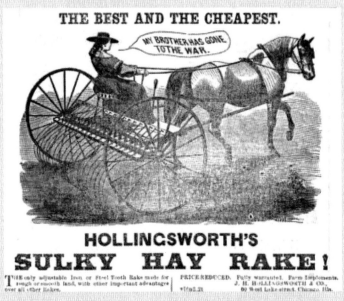

This advertisement for farm equipment spoke directly to the many women who were left to run the family farms. As the driver says, "My brother has gone to the war."

Websites

Websites active at the time of publication

Growing a Nation. Follow the story of American agriculture at agclassroom.org/gan/index.htm.

The Lincoln Log. A searchable daily chronology of Lincoln's activities. thelincolnlog.org/.

Lincoln's Cottage. Learn how the Lincolns spent their summers while living in Washington, DC. lincolncottage.org.

Mr. Lincoln's White House. See what life was like when the Lincolns lived in the White House. mrlincolnswhitehouse.org.

Selected Bibliography

All quotations used in the book can be found in the following sources marked with an asterisk.

*Basler, Roy P., editor; Marion Dolores Pratt and Lloyd A. Dunlap, assistant editors. *Collected Works of Abraham Lincoln*. New Brunswick, NJ: Rutgers University Press, 1953. Digitized in Ann Arbor, Michigan: University of Michigan Digital Library Production Services, 2001, quod.lib.umich.edu/l/lincoln/lincoln1/1:8?rgn=div1;view=fulltext.

*Carpenter, Francis B. *Six Months at the White House with Abraham Lincoln*. New York: Hurd & Houghton, 1866.

Donald, David Herbert. *Lincoln*. New York: Simon & Schuster Paperbacks, 1995.

Edwards, Everett E. "Lincoln's Attitude Toward Farm Problems." United States Department of Agriculture Bureau of Agricultural Economics, Washington DC, United States Department of Agriculture, Dec. 15, 1933.

Herndon, William H. *Herndon's Lincoln; The True Story of A Great Life*, vols. 1 and 2. Originally published in 1888. Reprinted in London: Forgotten Books, 2015.

Holzer, Harold, and Norton Garfinkle. *A Just and Generous Nation: Abraham Lincoln and the Fight for American Opportunity*. New York: Basic Books, 2015.

Hurt, R. Douglas. *Food and Agriculture during the Civil War*. Santa Barbara: Praeger, 2016.

Ross, Earle, D. "Lincoln and Agriculture." *Agricultural History*, vol. 3, no. 2. Fargo, ND: Agricultural History Society, April, 1929. Accessed online Core Historical Literature of Agriculture, Cornell University Mann Library, chla.library.cornell.edu/cgi/t/text/text-idx?c=chla;id no=5077685_4132_002.

*Wilson, Douglas, L., Rodney O. Davis, and Terry Wilson. *Herndon's Informants: Letters, Interviews, and Statements about Abraham Lincoln*. Urbana, Illinois: University of Illinois Press, 1998.

Winkle, Kenneth J. *Lincoln's Citadel: The Civil War in Washington, DC*. New York: W. W. Norton, 2013.

*Wisconsin State Agricultural Society. *Transactions of the Wisconsin State Agricultural Society, with Reports of County Societies, and Kindred Associations*, vol. 5. Madison, Wisconsin: Carpenter and Hyer, Printers, Patriot Office, 1858–1859. University of Wisconsin Digital Collection, digital.library.wisc.edu/1711.dl/WI.WSASv05.

Woolley, John T. and Gerhard Peters. The American Presidency Project. Updated October 20, 2018. presidency.ucsb.edu/.

To Kate and Greg, who, like Lincoln,
strive to make the world a better place
　　　—PT

For all those who work with their hands and
minds to feed the world
　　　—SI

Picture Credits

Library of Congress Prints and Photographs Division, LC-USZ62-2279-3a05993u: 40; LC-USZC4-2472: 41; LOT 12359-1G: 42; LC-DIG-ppmsca-22982: 44; LC-DIG-ppmsca-59361: 45; LC-USZ62-59908: 46 (left).

Reprinted from *Prairie Farmer*. Used with permission: 46 (right).

Calkins Creek
An imprint of Boyds Mills & Kane, a division of Astra Publishing House
calkinscreekbooks.com

Printed in China

ISBN: 978-1-68437-153-2 (hc) • 978-1-63592-370-4 (eBook)
Library of Congress Control Number: 2020933233

First edition
10 9 8 7 6 5 4 3 2 1

Design by Barbara Grzeslo
The type is set in ITC Officiano Sans.
The illustrations were done in gouache, acrylic, and ink and finished digitally.